Backyard HEROES

Rufus Bellamy

Crabtree Publishing Company
www.crabtreebooks.com

Author: Rufus Bellamy
Editor: Crystal Sikkens
Project coordinator: Kathy Middleton
Production coordinator: Ken Wright
Prepress technician: Margaret Amy Salter
Series consultant: Gill Matthews

Picture credits:
Dreamstime: Thomas Dobner 5t,
   Nadezda Pyastolova 19, Nitipong Ballapavanich 2, 4t, 8t,
   16t, 18t, Lee Daniels 3, 6, 11b, 22–23, Clayton Hansen 10t,
   Sandy Manter 8, Pavlo Maydikov 13, Dean Murray 12t,
   Dieter Spears 20
Istockphoto: (Cover), Dean Murray
Shutterstock: Cover, Goran Cakmazovic 5b, Peter Clark 17t,
   Steven Collins 7b, David Davis 11t, Arlene Jean Gee 9b,
   Karen Givens 4, Lukás Hejtman 15t,
   Jan van der Hoeven 21b, Iperl 7t,
   Johnnychaos 9t, Cathy Keifer 21t, Alexey Khromushin 15b,
   Steve Mann 16, Martha Marks 17b, Gyula Matics 12b,
   Steve McWilliam 18b, Gordana Sermek 10b,
   Juris Sturainis 14

Library and Archives Canada Cataloguing in Publication

Bellamy, Rufus
   Backyard heroes / Rufus Bellamy.

(Crabtree connections)
Includes index.
ISBN 978-0-7787-9953-5 (bound).--ISBN 978-0-7787-9975-7 (pbk.)

   1. Garden animals--Juvenile literature. I. Title.
II. Series: Crabtree connections

QL119.B44 2010   j591.75'54   C2010-901509-6

Library of Congress Cataloging-in-Publication Data

Bellamy, Rufus.
   Backyard heroes / Rufus Bellamy.
      p. cm. -- (Crabtree connections)
   Includes index.
   ISBN 978-0-7787-9975-7 (pbk. : alk. paper) -- ISBN 978-0-7787-9953-5
   (reinforced library binding : alk. paper)
   1. Garden animals--Juvenile literature. I. Title. II. Series.

QL119.B4523 2011
591.75'54--dc22

                                                2010008052

Crabtree Publishing Company
www.crabtreebooks.com   1-800-387-7650
Copyright © 2011 **CRABTREE PUBLISHING COMPANY.**
All rights reserved. No part of this publication may be reproduced, stored in a retrieval system or be transmitted in any form or by any means, electronic, mechanical, photocopying, recording, or otherwise, without the prior written permission of Crabtree Publishing Company. Published in the United Kingdom in 2009 by A & C Black Publishers Ltd. The right of the author of this work has been asserted.

Printed in the U.S.A./062010/WO20100815

Published in Canada
Crabtree Publishing
616 Welland Ave.
St. Catharines, Ontario
L2M 5V6

Published in the United States
Crabtree Publishing
PMB 59051
350 Fifth Avenue, 59th Floor
New York, New York 10118

Contents

Backyard Heroes

Backyards, parks, and even schoolyards are full of amazing animals and plants doing amazing things. In this book you'll get to meet some of the wildlife "action heroes" that live near your home. You'll discover just what they're up to and find out why they are so important.

Wildlife homes

Backyards and other open spaces around houses are really important for wildlife. They provide places where plants can grow and where animals can make a home and find food. Many animals and plants are threatened, so it is important that backyards are wildlife-friendly. If your backyard is large enough, leave an overgrown wild area—small creatures will soon move in.

Some birds, such as the killdeer, build nests on gravel and in open fields.

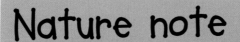

Nature note

Feeding birds is one way in which people can help wildlife. This is important when the weather is cold and food is hard to find.

Lovely ladybugs

Ladybugs eat pests, such as aphids, that attack backyard plants. In the winter, these spotted backyard heroes often sleep bunched together in little groups.

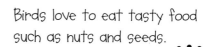

Birds love to eat tasty food such as nuts and seeds.

Ladybugs are a backyard's best friend.

Green Food

From the leaves on the trees to the grass on the lawn, backyards are full of greenery. All these green plants can do something amazing. They can make their own food.

Green plants use energy from the Sun to turn water and a gas called **carbon dioxide** into a type of sugar. They use this as food so they can live and grow. Carbon dioxide gets into a plant's leaves from the air. Water is taken in from the soil by its **roots**.

Precious plants

Animals can't make their own food. They eat plants, or they eat animals that eat plants. This means that all animals, including people, rely on green plants to survive.

Nature note

Trees have to lift water all the way up to their leaves. A big tree, such as an oak, can drink enough water in a day to fill a large bathtub.

Green plants and trees
are real backyard heroes.

Some leaves become red and
yellow in the fall. Other leaves
change from green to brown.

Color changes

Green plants are
green because they
have a chemical called
chlorophyll in their leaves.
Chlorophyll lets them
capture the energy of
the Sun. In fall, leaves
change color as their
chlorophyll disappears.

Marvelous Munchers

Backyard plants are a feast for many animals.
Slugs eat lettuce and rabbits nibble grass,
while birds peck the seeds, fruit, and berries
from all kinds of flowers, shrubs, and trees.

Important eaters

When an animal eats
a plant's berries or fruit,
it can be a good thing.
The fruit contains seeds
from which new plants
grow. Many animals
help spread out the
seeds through their
waste, or poop.

Animals that only eat plants, such as rabbits, are called herbivores.

Nature note

Squirrels eat nuts such as acorns from oak trees. They use their sharp teeth to break open the shells. In fall, they collect nuts and store them in holes. They dig the nuts up again when food is scarce.

Amazing aphids

Aphids are a real pest in the backyard because they eat backyard plants, such as roses. But aphids have an amazing secret. They produce something called honeydew. This is sweet and is eaten by many insects and other animals.

Butterflies lay eggs on plants so the caterpillars that hatch from the eggs can eat the leaves.

9

Hungry Hunters

The world outside your window is full of hungry hunters. Birds of prey is a term given to birds, such as eagles, hawks, and owls, that hunt animals for food. The peregrine falcon is a bird of prey famous for its steep, fast dives to capture an animal.

An owl's excellent eyesight can help it hunt in the dark.

Nature note

Spiders are amazing hunters. They make super-strong spider silk in their bodies and use it to spin webs to trap flies.

Expert hunters

Many animals have skills that make them good hunters, such as a strong sense of smell or excellent hearing. The herring gull has a special skill. It drops mussels onto rocks to break the shells and eat the animals inside.

Animals that hunt and eat other animals are called predators. The animals they catch are called prey.

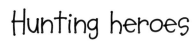
This moth is hard to see because it looks like the bark of the tree it is sitting on.

Hunting heroes

If there were no predators, there would be too many of the animals that usually get eaten. That's why gardeners love ladybugs, lacewings, and spined soldier bugs. They help keep down the number of backyard pests. Some animals have markings which frighten hunters away. Others have patterns and colors that camouflage them, or make it difficult for hunters to see them.

Important Insects

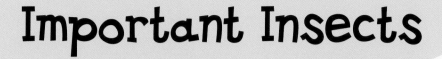

On a warm summer day the air outside is full of action. Bees and other insects buzz around looking for food. Many are searching for the sweet **nectar** and powdery **pollen** that is found inside flowers.

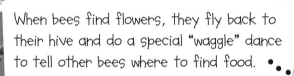

When bees find flowers, they fly back to their hive and do a special "waggle" dance to tell other bees where to find food.

Flowers need insects

When an insect goes inside a flower to look for food, pollen rubs off onto its body. As it flies around, the insect carries this pollen to other flowers.

If the insect passes pollen between two flowers of the same type, an amazing thing can happen: the flowers can start to make seeds from which new plants can grow. That's one reason why insects are real backyard heroes. Insects are so important, many gardeners try to attract them by planting flowers that provide nectar.

Butterflies love plants such as buddleias. That's why buddleias are known as the butterfly bush.

Nature note

Many flowers have patterns on their petals that only insects can see. The patterns attract insects. Insects can see these patterns because their eyes can see different types of light than ours.

Amazing Movers

You often only see the animals that live near your home when they move. They could be in search of food, escaping from a predator, or looking for a **mate**. Some amazing movers live in backyards.

Mega movers

A mole could tunnel half way across a soccer field in just one day! Snails and slugs don't have any legs, but can crawl up walls. They produce a sticky slime that lets them do this. It's this slime that makes the trails they leave behind. Bats are also amazing movers. They fly at night and catch tiny fast-moving insects in the dark.

Snails are amazing climbers! This snail is traveling up a steep plant stem.

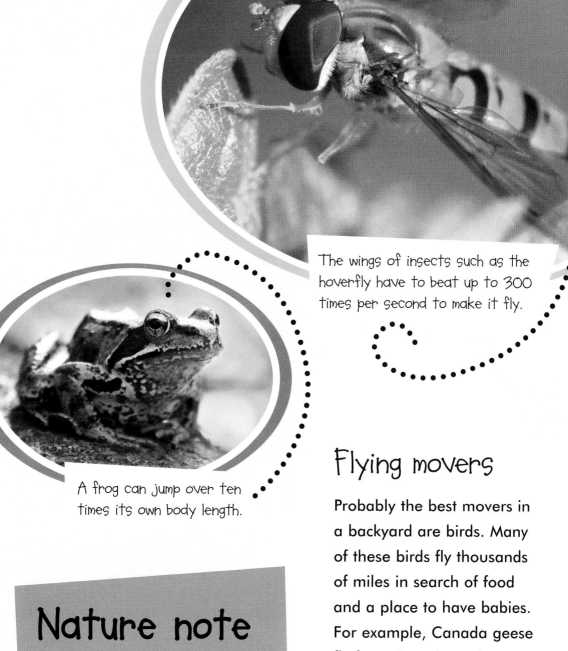

The wings of insects such as the hoverfly have to beat up to 300 times per second to make it fly.

A frog can jump over ten times its own body length.

Flying movers

Probably the best movers in a backyard are birds. Many of these birds fly thousands of miles in search of food and a place to have babies. For example, Canada geese fly from Canada to the United States and Mexico and back. This type of movement is called **migration**.

Nature note

You can see where animals have moved by looking for their prints or tracks. These can usually be found in soft earth.

Heroic Homemakers

Many backyard animals make amazing homes. Barn swallows build nests made of mud. Mice, rabbits, and badgers are just some of the animals that dig to make homes underground.

Wildlife-friendly

Because wild animals like their homes to be hidden away, long grass and other "untidy" parts of a backyard, such as thick hedges and nettle patches, are important. They provide shelter for animals.

Untidy corners make good homes for many backyard animals.

Trees, such as the oak, are also important homes for many animals and plants. **Fungi** live among their roots and squirrels build nests called dreys in their branches.

Plants are also clever at making themselves at home in a backyard. Some tough plants, such as the dandelion, are able to grow in cracks in pathways.

Robins often make their nests in backyards.

A winter sleep

Some backyard animals such as groundhogs **hibernate** during the winter. This is like going into a very deep sleep. They dig holes in the ground to make warm nests.

Nature note

The area where an animal lives is called its **territory**. Many animals, such as robins, will fight each other to guard their territories.

17

Radical Recyclers

People are not the only ones who recycle waste so that it can be used again. In a backyard there are many recycling heroes.

These recyclers feed on dead and decaying plants and animals. They break these things down and release the **nutrients** they contain into the soil. Plants then use these nutrients to live and grow.

Wood lice are just one of many animals that eat rotting plant material.

Invisible workers

Microscopic bacteria do a lot of the work of breaking down dead things. Larger plants, such as mushrooms and other fungi, also break down old leaves and other plant material.

Wonderful worms

Worms are very important waste recyclers. They eat soil and dead and decaying plants. Worms produce **casts** that are full of nutrients and good for plants. Worms also mix up the soil, which is another way in which they help gardeners.

When you see a mushroom you only see a small part of it. The rest is made up of a web of tiny fibers, or roots, that spread out in the soil underneath it.

Extraordinary Offspring

Backyard activity is perhaps at its most exciting when a new offspring, or baby animal, arrives. When they are born, animals such as birds, mice, and rabbits are fed and cared for by their parents. But many animals, such as frogs and toads, must look after themselves.

Finding a mate

To have babies most animals must first attract a mate. They do this in many different ways. For example, many birds sing and grasshoppers make a chirping noise by rubbing their wings against their back legs.

When baby animals are born, they are at risk from predators.

pupa

butterfly

When a caterpillar changes into a butterfly, the change is called **metamorphosis**.

Growing and changing

Some animals change a lot as they grow. For example, butterflies lay eggs that hatch into caterpillars. Each caterpillar eats a lot of food, grows, and then forms a pupa, or chrysalis. An amazing change then occurs—the caterpillar becomes a beautiful butterfly.

Nature note

The cowbird lays its eggs in a nest belonging to another pair of birds. The new parents have to do the hard work of bringing up the baby cowbird.

Frogs hatch from eggs called spawn as tiny tadpoles. Over the next few months they grow front and back legs and lose their tails to become adults.

21

Glossary

carbon dioxide Gas found in air

cast Small pile of soil produced by an earthworm

chlorophyll Green pigment found in leaves

fungi Mushrooms and some molds are among the many types of fungi

hibernate To save energy and survive the winter by going into a deep sleep

mate One of a pair of animals of the same species (one male, one female) that get together to have offspring (babies)

metamorphosis The process by which an animal changes shape as it develops and grows

microscopic Too small to be seen with just the eye

migration The large-scale movement of animals in search of food, a place to breed, or warmer weather

nectar Sugary liquid plants make to attract insects

nutrients Chemicals plants and animals need to survive

pollen Powder made by the male parts of some plants

roots Plant parts that absorb water and nutrients

territory Area an animal occupies and defends

Further Information

Web sites

Find out more about the birds, animals, and insects in your backyard at:

www.backyardnature.net/

Find out how much you know about your backyard animals with a fun game at:

**www.sheppardsoftware.com/content/animals
/quizzes/kidscorner/animal_
games_backyard_flower_large.html**

Books

Animals in the Garden by Mari Schuh.
Capstone (2010).

Backyard Bugs by Jenny Vaughan.
Tick Tock Books (2009).

Living things in my back yard by
Bobbie Kalman. Crabtree Publishing (2008).

Index